HEAVY METAL IN THE
MIDDLE EAST AND AFRICA

D1295918

ISBN: 978-1-387-77019-9

Printed in the United States of America.

Cover photo by Skeeze; licensed under Creative Commons.
Title font licensed from Chris Vile.
Cover design by Beth Winegarner.

HEAVY METAL IN THE
MIDDLE EAST AND AFRICA

BETH WINEGARNER

TABLE OF CONTENTS

INTRODUCTION

I didn't set out to write about heavy metal in the Middle East and Africa. But when I was researching my last book, *The Columbine Effect*—particularly the parts about the Satanic Panic and heavy metal in the United States in the 1980s—I came across reports of bands in the Middle East experiencing a present-day Satanic Panic. I had lived through the U.S. version, and although there was a lot of fear and misinformation, no metal fans or musicians went to jail because of it. Ozzy Osbourne and Judas Priest went on trial amid the chaos, and Slayer was nearly blamed for a girl's murder, but the law was ultimately on their side.

That's not the case in the Middle East and parts of Africa, where laws against Satanism and blasphemy sometimes become an excuse for police to harass, imprison or torture metalheads. In my research I learned about Bassem Deaïbess, frontman for Lebanon band Blaakyum and former frontman for The Hourglass, a Syrian band, who'd been arrested twice—and dodged police many other times—for his involvement in metal scenes. After I blogged about his ordeals, he reached out to me, and we struck up an ongoing dialogue. We turn out to have a lot in common, especially a frustration with moral panics and governments who use those panics to distract from more serious issues.

As I got to know Deaïbess, I connected with others in Lebanon, and then more broadly, including many who'd faced police abuses. I wrote about moral panics and the mistreatment of metalheads for *PopMatters*, interviewed Deaïbess in more depth for *Invisible Oranges* when Blaakyum released a new album in 2012, and wrote about a cluster of metal fans in Cairo who were falsely arrested and imprisoned for Invisible Oranges in 2013.

Connecting with these metalheads on a personal level was, in many ways, reassuring. No community is a monolith but, in general, I found that we had a lot in common. Music is a huge part of our lives, and lots of us are ambitious, creative types who've been marginalized by mainstream culture. Many have an activist streak, sparked by government corruption, environmental devastation, social injustice and/or ongoing violence. Because of metal's ability to express and release negative emotions, it often becomes a kind of medicine for those who love it. It becomes easy to understand why folks living in war zones, or places where bombings and threats of violence are commonplace, would be drawn to heavy metal. And why they would refuse to give it up, even in the face of police harassment, or worse.

I wasn't the only Western writer exploring

these ideas. Banger Films' Sam Dunn and Scot Mc-Fadyen released their documentary *Global Metal* in 2007, and Mark Levine's book *Heavy Metal Islam* came out in 2008. While watching *Global Metal*, I was struck by a conspicuous absence: it didn't include any women musicians. I knew they had to be out there, so I started digging, particularly on a couple of Middle East metal websites, Metality and Jorzine. I reached out to dozens of bands, and began corresponding with several women musicians, hoping to write something about what it's like making this music regions where the deck is seemingly so stacked against them. Ultimately, those conversations wound up in a piece for the *New Yorker*. It ran at a time when mainstream stereotypes about Middle Eastern and Muslim women were very specific and very narrow—and didn't include, say, an Egyptian woman singing death growls or an Iranian woman fronting a metal band when it was illegal for women there to perform in public.

Learning about these bands can help us understand how the complicated, volatile political situations in the Middle East and North Africa affect everyday citizens, particularly young people—as well as how Western involvement has shaped those situations. I've stayed in touch with many of the musicians I've written about, sharing their horror at regional violence and Western xenophobia, including the Brexit vote and the election of Donald Trump. I often wish I could go visit them and talk face to face, share a drink, or give them hugs, but these regions aren't the safest places for a white, female journalist to travel alone.

When I decided I wanted to release this collection, I wanted to offer something that hadn't been published anywhere else. I learned about filmmaker Monzer Darwish, a Syrian metalhead who'd made *Syrian Metal is War*, a documentary about his country's metal scene and its efforts to hang on amid the civil war, and began talking with him online. Including him feels like coming full circle, especially since he interviewed Deaïbess for the film. As I'm putting the finishing touches on this book, the situation in Syria is getting worse—the U.S., U.K. and France are bombing targets in the region. Darwish left the country in 2014, but his family and many friends are still there.

I want to acknowledge that, as a white Westerner, I am writing about cultures and history that are not my own, and doing so from a perspective of safety and privilege. I am likely to have gotten things wrong, or omitted important details. For the most part, I have tried to be a conduit for these musicians and fans to tell their own stories. They deserve to have their voices and music heard, and they also deserve safety, prosperity and hope. I urge you to read more about them, buy their albums and, if you're in a position to do so, give them a wider platform.

In addition, a portion of the proceeds from this

book will go toward Syrian Eyes, a nonprofit in Lebanon that provides shelter and aid to Syrian refugees. Lebanon has taken in more than a million Syrian refugees since the war began, according to the UN Refugee Agency.

Getting to know these metalheads has deepened my understanding of why this music is so important to so many of us around the world. And it has strengthened my anger and opposition to any government, law or morality group that seeks to separate metalheads from the music that helps them cope with their most difficult feelings and circumstances.

"You reign in terror as the world around you falls, succumbing at your feet/But never again shall I surrender my will to the ignorant and meek/The path is laid and I am on my way/Across the line of fear." — *Blaakyum, 2016*

THE HEAVY METAL WITCH HUNT LIVES ON

June 2012

The first frenetic riffs of Kaoteon's set shook the Beirut crowd as a handful of undercover police entered the club with automatic rifles.

Cops took the band hostage, locked them in the trunks of unmarked cars, and interrogated them for days, shuttling them from one location to another. A dozen others were arrested at the gig, including fans and bar managers. Their crime? Backing music that leaders believe is a front for Satanism.

"They were after the obscure music we played and the mysterious metal culture we were spreading," guitarist Anthony Kaoteon told me. "The people running the game in the government are not educated enough to understand their neighbors ... At least all of them ignorant bastards can agree on having a common enemy, and that is loud, distorted music played by obscure musicians who don't buy their bullshit."

It was 20 December 2003. It wasn't the first

Anthony Kaoteon of Kaoteon. Photo courtesy the band.

time police in Lebanon had gone after heavy metal, and it wouldn't be the last.

Roughly 60 percent of Lebanon is Muslim, but its place on the Mediterranean and its period of

French control after World War I have contributed to Lebanon's striking cultural and religious diversity. Its politics, both internally and in relationship with neighboring countries, are complex as a result. The country is home to a relatively free media and adopted Internet technology early.

However, it has also staged at least three attacks on heavy metal culture. The most recent was last September, when Beirut police rounded up eight metalheads. They sought a dozen more, including concert promoter Elia Mssawir, who had the good fortune to be vacationing in Istanbul when the cops came calling. The charges against Mssawir were dropped before he returned home, but those in custody were charged with blasphemy and drug consumption, according to military court judge Saqr Saqr.

"They belong to an organization that promotes insulting religious rites, which is against the law, and of course there are rituals which they practice," Saqr Saqr told NOW Lebanon.

After 16 years of persecution, Lebanese metalheads have grown used to it. The trouble began in 1996, when a government committee blacklisted heavy metal music for its alleged ties to the 1994 suicide of a high-ranking military officer's son. Nirvana—blamed for suicides after frontman Kurt Cobain shot himself—was also verboten. Before the boy's death, heavy metal plastered the Lebanese airwaves. After, metalheads who ran afoul of police were fair game.

Bassem Deaïbess, frontman for Lebanon's Blaakyum, spent a frigid night in a Beirut jail in 1996 for the crime of being a Metallica fan. The next day, he was asked: "Do you practice Nirvana? Do you worship the Devil? What would you do if you were given a cat?" (Police in many Arab nations are puzzlingly convinced that Satanists like to hurt felines.) He was relatively lucky; others received beatings or haircuts at the hands of police.

When Deaïbess, a Christian, showed his interrogator the rosary around his wrist, he was accused of wearing it as "camouflage." After signing papers promising that he would not listen to Nirvana or worship the Devil, he was released—only to be arrested again in 2007 for operating a heavy-metal-friendly pub in Beirut.

Each wave of arrests has been an effort by Lebanese leaders to distract the public from a political crisis, such as the end of the Syrian occupation in 2005 or increasing gas prices in 2002, Deaïbess said. "I firmly believe that every time the government needs to distract people from important issues, they will start an attack on metalheads. We are always the scapegoat of this rotten society."

After the arrests in 2002 and 2003, many metal musicians fled Lebanon for good, weakening the scene. "[Arrests] will happen again. The Lebanese metal community is too weak right now to do much about it. I hope we'll have enough good records that are supported internationally, so that our voice is so loud they can't shut it out anymore," Kaoteon said.

The Devil's Music

Around the world, heavy metal has been aligned with Satanism in the minds of mainstream culture since Led Zeppelin guitarist Jimmy Page bought Aleister Crowley's Loch Ness mansion, or perhaps even since Robert Johnson, whose blues became the bedrock of metal, struck his mythical deal with the Devil. Given their rebellious nature, many metal musicians have embraced the iconography of Satanism—the inverted crosses, the pentagrams, the fake blood—in the same way kids dress up as ghosts and vampires on Halloween, for theatrics and to be part of the fun.

At the height of the Satanic Panic in the '80s and early '90s, many Americans believed that heavy metal music could drive listeners to the occult, suicide, or even murder, as in the case of the recently released West Memphis Three. Anti-heavy-metal action in America culminated with "parental advisory" stickers, prompted by the PMRC's crusade against a blacklist of objectionable music—much of it heavy metal.

In most places, music fans can't be arrested for their listening habits alone. But in countries dominated by faith, particularly those with anti-blasphemy laws, officials don't appreciate the difference between metal's "Satanic" theatrics and occasional—but rare—violence committed by so-called "Devil worshippers." They've used such laws to lash out at metal musicians and fans. For metalheads in these places, the Satanic Panic is far from over.

The most brutal attacks to date took place this March in Iraq, where a dozen or more emo youth were stoned to death after the Interior Ministry falsely connected emo culture with Satanism. But the attackers—allegedly militia—weren't splitting hairs. Anyone who dressed in black or had unconventional hair, piercings, or tattoos was a target. A Mosul heavy-metal musician told the Human Rights Watch that two of his bandmates had been killed in the attacks.

Why would young people champion a genre of music that risks their freedom or personal safety? For most metalheads, this is more than entertainment; they're part of a tribe, an extension of themselves.

"A Jordanian metal musician said that metal was not a style of music you choose, it chooses YOU," said Jeremy Wallach, co-editor of *Metal Rules the Globe*, a collection of essays on metal in places such as Indonesia, Malaysia, Nepal, and Easter Island. "Heavy metal fans are not casual fans. Social scientists are finally starting to realize how much the role of music has been underestimated in human history, including recent history."

In many countries, heavy metal has represented everything that conservative, religiously traditional nations hope to resist: globalization, particularly Westernization; freedom of speech and ideas; democracy. Researchers are investigating heavy metal's place in the fall of the Soviet Union and the democratic revolutions in Eastern Europe. It was also there for the Arab Spring, Wallach said.

"Metal just fits the anger, even desperation and disgust that so many young people feel—there really is no genre of music that captures these feelings the way extreme metal does," Mark Levine, author of *Heavy Metal Islam*, told me. "Moreover, since until recently it was quite dangerous to take on regimes directly, singing brutally was a good way to avoid directly opening oneself up to attacks by the government for subversive lyrics, since hardly anyone who's not a metal fan could understand brutal lyrics sung in English!"

It's no wonder that countries on the brink of profound change might want to rub out heavy metal. Police surveillance and unpredictable arrests—of even a few people—can have a chilling effect on a whole nation, as happened in Lebanon. No metalheads understand this chilling effect better than those in Egypt—the site of the worst such arrests in history.

The Day the Music Died

Young people in Cairo will never forget 22 January 1997. That night, as more than 100 metalheads headed to bed, Egyptian police burst into their homes. Most were regulars at a place called the Baron's Palace, an abandoned villa turned illegal hangout for the city's metalheads. After the arrests, one Egyptian paper claimed the villa was "filled with tattooed, devil-worshipping youths holding orgies, skinning cats, and writing their names in rats' blood on the palace walls," according to Levine.

While police rounded up their suspects, they also seized "evidence," including CDs and cassettes, posters, and black t-shirts—heavy metal or not. Many of these kids (as young as 13) spent at least two weeks in jail, some as long as 45 days. During that time, they were interrogated, fielding questions from "Do you participate in pagan rituals?" to "Do you skin cats?" Egyptian leader Sheikh Nars Farid Wassil demanded they repent or be executed for apostasy. After finding little evidence against them, a public prosecutor ordered their release.

Levine linked the 1997 crackdown to a rise in extremist activity in Egypt, one which the government struggled—and failed—to control; radical Islamists attacked tourist spots in Luxor later that year.

Although there have been no major arrests since, metalheads in Cairo remain cowed, perhaps because military police continue to supervise their gigs. Almost none would speak on the record to Levine, an experience I also faced.

The Forsaken Past

Moroccan leaders expecting to have a similarly chilling effect got more than they bargained for when they arrested 14 metal musicians and fans in February 2003 on charges of "possessing objects which infringe morals." Nine of the men, all in their early 20s to mid-30s, played in Casablanca metal bands Reborn, Infected Brain and Nekros. They were sentenced to between three months and a year in jail for their metal affiliations, especially for possessing skeletons, skulls, snakes and "diabolical" CDs.

Casablanca's cultural champions fought back. Journalists for the French-language TelQuel magazine skewered the judge for saying, "normal people go to concerts in a suit and tie," rather than the all-black outfits favored by metalheads. When the convicted men appealed their sentences, supporters—including families of the jailed—swarmed the courthouse in their defense.

Yousra Atmen, singer for Casablanca metal band Analgesia, was a 15-year-old high school student when the bust went down. At first, she thought the metalhead arrests were just a rumor.

"I found it so weird and couldn't understand. [But] a friend of mine didn't come to school for a few days at that time. He was a long-haired guitarist of a local band. He told me, later on, that he was arrested for some investigations about the music, and if it had a link with religion."

Moroccan authorities believed that heavy metal was a "Satanist movement" attempting to convert listeners away from Islam—a crime in the country. "They thought that these people drink blood and do rituals to call Satan through metal music," Atmen said.

Many noted that the Casablanca arrests came just as Islamic politicians were enjoying a surge in power in Morocco. At first, metalheads and their worried parents were frightened, according to Atmen. But soon, hard rock and heavy metal exploded in the country, thanks in part to the creation of the Boulevard Festival in 2006. The annual event draws local and international heavyweights such as Arch Enemy and Sepultura. The reigning king, Mohammad VI, is a sponsor.

Another key development in Morocco's understanding of heavy metal was Ahmed Boulane's 2007 film *Les Anges du Satan (Satan's Angels)*, detailing the 2003 arrests and the country's response. Boulane was effective in explaining that heavy metal is simply a style of music, not a religious movement, according to Atmen.

Those arrests are "the forsaken past," she said. "No one ever talks about it nowadays."

The Voice of Poland

Islam-dominated countries have by no means cornered the market on demonizing heavy metal. In 2010, officials in Russia's Belgorod region banned heavy metal concerts in order to protect "the spiritual safety" of the area. A South African rock and metal festival, RAMfest, was relocated from a Bloemfontein venue this spring after emails circulated claiming the festival's logo—a ram's head surrounded by lightning bolts and spears—celebrated Satanic and Illuminati ideals.

Over the past decade, Poland has hosted one of the biggest knock-down, drag-out fights between heavy metal and faith. While Poland celebrates freedom of expression, it's also illegal to make statements that "offend religious feeling." This law, which many Poles agree is overly subjective, has nailed more than one metal band for doing what they do best.

Norway's Gorgoroth brought its stage show to Kraków in 2004—a performance dubbed the "black mass", featuring naked women on crucifixes, sheep's heads on stakes, and 80 liters of sheep's blood. Police investigated them on religious-offense charges, confiscating footage of the show. Although Polish officials dropped their charges against Gorgoroth, the band was dumped from Nuclear Blast Records in the furor.

The next target was one of Poland's own: Adam Darski, who performs under the stage name Nergal as frontman of the blackened death metal band Behemoth. He identifies as a follower of Thelema, the spiritual path pioneered by notorious British occultist Aleister Crowley. Though Thelema is based on Egyptian spirituality and ceremonial magic, it's often mistakenly associated with Satanism.

That may be one reason why, when Darski took the stage in his hometown of Gdansk in September 2007, he destroyed a Bible mid-set. He said, "They call it the Holy Book. I call this the book of lies. Fuck the shit, fuck the hypocrisy." He also called the Catholic Church "the most murderous cult on the planet."

The incident might have gone unnoticed, if not for the ultraconservative Ryszard Nowak, leader of the All-Polish Committee for Defense Against Sects. Nowak had provided Polish political leaders with a list of bands who "promoted Satanism". He sued Darski over the Bible-destroying incident, invoking the "offending religious feeling" clause. In August 2011, a judge acquitted Darski, defending the singer's freedom-of-speech rights.

"I'm so glad to see that intelligence won over religious fanatics in my home country," Darski said in a statement on Behemoth's website. "There's still so much work to be done to make things right. The battle is won, but the war ain't over."

He wasn't wrong. By the time of his acquittal, Darski's celebrity in Poland had grown, thanks in part to his role as a judge on the reality-TV show

The Voice of Poland. The fact that such an icon of anti-Catholic sentiment appeared on national television chafed many in the religious community. Shortly after the series premiered in September, the Polish Catholic Association of Journalists stated, "The participation of Adam Darski—a Satanist and outspoken enemy of Christian values—contradicts the missionary nature of Polish television."

Bishop Wieslaw Mering, head of the Catholic diocese of Wlocawek in northern Poland, got in on the action. In a public statement, he called Darski "a blasphemer, Satanist, and lover of evil incarnate", and claimed that his role on TV would allow him to "spread his poisonous teachings". Mering urged Poles to stop paying money to the television channel airing the program.

In the middle of the uproar, Darski appeared on the cover of Polish *Newsweek*, wrapped in a Polish flag, naked from the waist up, and bearing a sword in his right hand. "God. Horror. Fatherland.," read the cover headline.

Neither the controversy nor the publicity cowed Darski. When Behemoth performed in Warsaw on 1 October, two guitarists from their opening band, Times New Roman, appeared onstage in wheelchairs. Dressed as a priest, Darski pretended to heal and bless them. They rose from their wheelchairs and Behemoth began to perform.

Voice of Poland producers couldn't take it anymore. After the "healing" stunt, they announced that

Darski would not return to judge a second season of the show. Mering called his opposition to Darski—and what Mering described as "promotion of Satanism in the public media"—one of his diocese's highlights of the year.

"Taking the Fight to Them"

Whether it's an upstart metal band in Lebanon or a Polish rocker recognized around the world, many of these musicians and their fans have risked everything to pursue the music they love. As Western popular culture makes its way into these countries—hastened by social media— is the tide turning? Will metalheads find ways to perform and enjoy heavy metal freely?

Poland watched closely as the row between Darski and his religious foes played out. Darski lost a job; in that way, the conservatives won. However, cases in which the country's "offending religious feeling" clause is enforced are rare—and frequently targeted at celebrities such as Darski, according to Brian Porter-Szücs, author of Faith and Fatherland: Catholicism, Modernity, and Poland. "In fact, it appears to be unenforceable in practice. More important is probably the way it creates space for right-wing activists to attack their opponents an legal grounds, and this does have a certain chilling effect on public discussion of the Catholic Church's role in Poland," he said.

Today, there is a small but growing backlash against the law, led by Polish legislator Janusz Palikot, because it's so subjective. Palikot has submitted a proposal to overturn it, backed by a growing number of young and urban Poles, according to Porter-Szücs—who added that it's not likely to pass.

He believes Darski will be able to transform the controversy into bigger success, an experience Behemoth shares with Kaoteon. Ten days after Beirut police released the band from custody, Kaoteon entered the studio and recorded their demo, *Provenance of Hatred.* That album, and the story of their incarceration, have made a name for the band in Lebanon and beyond, Anthony Kaoteon said.

While some may be able to spin run-ins with political and religious leaders into notoriety, that leaves lesser known musicians and fans vulnerable. Could Morocco's success in overturning the false link between heavy metal and Satanism work elsewhere—or does it take a thriving metal scene, backed by a savvy population, to force change? And what can musicians and fans in ultra-restrictive nations such as Iran, where all popular music is heavily policed and metalheads are routinely jailed, do to reverse the threats they face?

When I asked Wallach how heavy metal communities could change things, he responded glibly, "Metalheads don't care what people think." But that clearly isn't true everywhere: Mssawir appeared on a Lebanese Geraldo Rivera-style talk show recently to dispute the conflation of heavy metal and Satanism. Afterward, he received emails from parents, thanking him for the relief they felt about their teenagers' listening habits.

That approach is the right one, said Deaïbess. "We are planning on taking the fight to them. We will be the ones steering the issue. We want to get this ignorant society off our backs once and for all."

INTERVIEW:
BASSEM DEAÏBESS OF
LEBANON'S BLAAKYUM

February 2012

Blaakyum frontman Bassem Deaïbess was born in Beirut in 1977, in the midst of a 15-year civil war. When he was 3, his family left for Qatar, which was relatively peaceful and still under British cultural influence. Despite being a Christian, in Qatar Deaïbess was forced to memorize the Koran and Islamic prayers, was forbidden to wear a cross, and was mocked by other students.

Despite the ongoing war, he returned to Lebanon each summer. "Sometimes we'd get stuck in my grandfather's house, since artillery were located few meters away," he says. "The sound of bombshells dropping, and machine guns that light up the sky at night, are all vivid memories."

Deaïbess began to study theology, but his parents also turned him on to Lebanese folk music, Persian pop, and the Beatles. By his last year in Qatar, he had become an accomplished breakdancer and

Bassem Deaïbess of Blaakyum.

joined a Christian youth group, where he would create and perform live shows set to the music of Michael Jackson. He also began to play drums and acoustic guitar. Then a nun told him he could play music and still serve God.

He formed Blaakyum in 1995, four years after he returned to Lebanon for good. Iron Maiden, Metallica, Testament, Dream Theater, Annihilator, Helstar, Nevermore, Opeth, and Deep Purple were major influences. The band played its first gig January 13, 1996, in Beirut.

That year, the Lebanese government blacklisted many heavy metal bands and began arresting musicians and fans. Another round of arrests followed in 2002, and another in 2011. Deaïbess was detained twice. I met Deaïbess online in 2011 after writing about the latest wave of Lebanese metalhead arrests on my blog, *Backward Messages*.

This year, on the anniversary of Blaakyum's first gig, its album *Lord of the Night* was released. The current lineup includes Rany Battikh on bass, Elias Njeim ("The Shredder of Lebanon") on lead guitar, and Jad Feitroui on drums.

Lord of the Night is a subgenre-hopping romp through metal, with lyrics of political unrest and defiance. Given Deaïbess's upbringing and experiences—Middle-East strife, a family of conservative Christians and Communists, doing jail time for his love of metal—it could hardly be any other way.

Q: How did you discover heavy metal music?

A: Metal was big in Lebanon, especially during the '80s. When I came back to Lebanon, it was all over the radio. You could hear Metallica, Iron Maiden, and Nirvana almost every day. My real introduction came in 1993 when my cousin gave me two cassette tapes: the Scorpions' Crazy World and a Body Count mixed tape. This was a clever way to initiate me to metal, since I was more of a pop/hip-hop/rap person. A few weeks later I bought my first rock tape: Guns N' Roses' *Use Your Illusion I&II*. Metallica's *Black Album* followed, then Iron Maiden's *Fear Of The Dark*, and there, I was in love.

Q: When did you start playing heavy metal?

A: At Don Bosco [the Christian youth group], I learned guitar and started messing around with classics. In 1994, I saw a Les Paul and asked my father to buy it for me. I was so happy that I had a guitar that looked like Slash's! But I was disappointed when I did not hear any distortion coming out of it. Back then, where I lived, no one played metal, and no one knew about distortion. One day, while I had my guitar plugged into an old Sanyo stereo, I was playing the music so loud, I had to crank up the volume to the max and there ... magic! I heard a distorted guitar. I was so happy, but I probably made all the neighbors angry!

Q: What is the Lebanese heavy metal scene like?

A: Compared to a population of 4 million, it is huge! Small gigs in pubs can have up to 300 people, and we have an average of at least one every month. We have over 50 bands in all kinds of genres, including post-rock and post-metal. We have 4 bands, including Blaakyum, who have gigged outside Lebanon.

In 1997, we had our first big multi-local festival called, simply, "Rock Concert," with about 1,500 in attendance. "Rock Concert II" had more. In 2001, a series of metal festivals called "Rock Nation" started and was held each year until 2008. It had around

2,500 attending. After the attacks on metal, festivals started seeing smaller and smaller numbers, but the average is around 1,000 during summer. We have at least one metal fest every year.

On the other hand, we have zero support. We do not have facilities to work in, and we do not have opportunities to grasp. Being in a metal band means spending more money on the band than you can ever make even from your regular job. It is a life of sacrifice, and we do it simply because we love this form of art.

Q: What was the Lebanese atmosphere around heavy metal music when you started playing? How has it changed since then?

A: In 1994, a young boy committed suicide, and newspapers started talking about the dangers of hard rock music. In 1995, a few religious groups and a Christian TV channel started an organized campaign against this "dangerous" form of music. By 1996, the government had adopted the campaign and the persecution started. People would get caught simply for having long hair and/or dressing in black. A blacklist of most metal bands, along with Nirvana, was established by the Lebanese control committee, and suddenly it became "illegal" to possess or buy metal. When a blacklist is put together, the committee then sends it to the customs office around the country and to the border offices, airports, etc. We were forced to evade police or military checkpoints.

I was arrested while at the gate of my university. Many others were arrested. Concerts were stopped. It continued until 1998, when it slowly started to fade away and people started forgetting. The whole metal and "Satanic music" issue rose again, and 2002 was hell on earth for us. Arrests were more violent, people were beaten up, some people were kicked out of their neighborhoods, and some even had to leave the country.

During the first wave, many metal bands made it through, like Cannibal Corpse and other extreme music. The main bands that were banned were the most famous like Iron Maiden, Metallica, Megadeth, Slayer, and definitely the "evil" Nirvana. By 2002, all metal music was forbidden.

The severity of attacks faded by 2004, but only disappeared after the assassination of the businessman [and former Prime Minister] Rafik Al Hariri in 2005. That led Syrian troops to leave Lebanon for good, and the Lebanese political system got so busy with the chaos that no one had time to attack metal music.

In 2011, a new wave of attacks started, but this time it was weak—because Lebanon had stopped being a proper police state, because the economic and political situations were too heavy for people to get interested, and because it seems to most that the police have the situation under control.

This time, we are planning on bringing the fight

to them. We will be the ones steering the issue again, as we want to get this ignorant society off our back once and for all.

Q: You were arrested twice by Lebanese authorities, for being a metalhead, basically. Can you describe those arrests?

A: The first time, I was arrested by the military police, which in itself is against the law! That was in 1996. There was a checkpoint right before the university gate, and I was stopped there. They asked me if I like Nirvana. I said no. They asked me if I like Metallica and I said yes—and that was enough, with my long hair and black clothes, to be detained. I was sent to a dungeon-like prison. When the officer filled the form, the "charge" line was left empty. I was taken for two days. Luckily, they didn't cut my hair, but others were less fortunate.

It was freezing cold. I had to sleep with half my body covered with my jacket while the other half froze. I'd wake up few minutes later to switch my jacket to the other side ... I barely slept. The next day, I was taken to the investigator's office. After some insults and humiliation, he started asking questions like, "do you practice Nirvana?" The official opinion was that "Nirvana" was a form of death-loving plague that makes people commit suicide if they listen to "Nirvana" music—which was anything heavy!

He later asked me about worshiping the devil, and I showed him my wrist, which had a rosary around it. His reply was, "This is a camouflage, you won't fool me with it!" Then he asked me what would I do if I was given a cat! Dumb stuff like that. By the end, he made me sign a paper stating that I would not indulge in Nirvana nor worship the Devil. I was let out by the evening.

The second time was in 2007. The secret intelligence came to the metal/rock pub I ran at the time, asked me to go with them for questioning, and I did. They asked almost the same questions. What saved me was the fact that I had a priest who'd attended concerts [at the pub] with a bunch of guys from his church, and we were good friends.

Q: How many others have been arrested for the same things?

A: The thing is, there is no law banning metal, nor even Satanism. So most of the time there is no charge, as none of those arrested were caught in any immoral situation, nor were they blaspheming! Most detentions went on for a maximum of three days. Some were beaten, others only insulted. It all depended on the officer who interrogated them.

One band, Kaoteon, had people break into their concert with weapons—probably secret police of the anti-terrorism regiment. They took the musicians, put them in civil car trunks, and drove them to an unknown destination, where they were held and interrogated. The band was held because in Arabic, Shaitan means Satan, and Shaiatinon means a bunch of devils. The officials thought Kaoteon is read Shaotenon, and considered them Satanists.

Q: Why do you think Lebanese authorities went after heavy-metal musicians?

A: The Christian Church here is so powerful, especially the Catholic Maronite Church, and has a huge influence on politics. So do the Islamic religious institutions. The whole thing was led by people (priests, institutions) from the church, though not the church itself.

Many benefited from these attacks. The authorities found an opportunity to distract the public from the essential issues and the corruption they were leading against the Lebanese people, and to come across as the protector of society—which is not the case, since to this day police fail to capture criminals, or solve any significant security issue. Journalists created fictional stories to gain money and fame.

I firmly believe that every time the government needs to distract people from important issues, they will start an attack on metalheads. We are always the scapegoat of this rotten society.

Q: How did these arrests affect the heavy-metal scene in Lebanon?

A: It damaged the scene considerably. It's almost impossible to find a proper venue to perform, because most refuse to let metal bands play. We have to accept playing in the few less-than-average venues that accept us. It is thanks to the Internet that the scene still exists, as government cannot control that ... yet!

Q: What made 2012 the right time to produce and release *Lord of the Night*?

A: It wasn't. We intended to record and release by the end of 2008. We faced two major problems: the band was forced to part with our drummer, George Najjarian, because he signed a contract with a venue and was not allowed to perform anywhere else. Later we fired the guitarist because of musical differences. It took us a whole year to find a new lineup. Later on, we faced a problem with the production house (New Wave Production), as it got too occupied with mainstream Arabic and pop production, and didn't have time for us— especially because we'd won the production time when we won the Lebanese Global Battle of the Bands, so we were not paying customers.

We recorded the album three times. The first was a live recording to check how our sound will turn out. After the lineup changes, our producer realized that he was too busy for us and referred us to [another studio]. After finishing the whole album using VST (digitally recorded) drums and digital guitar effects, we felt it was not really authentic. We decided to re-record everything from scratch. At first I opposed the idea, as I realized it would take an awful lot of time, but I am glad the guys convinced me—the sound is very much raw and authentic.

Q: Can you talk a little about the album itself?

A: Originally, Blaakyum intended to release a double album that was a complete story of the Black Family over three generations. It included the adventures of Sir Edward Black in "Part One: The Gate" and his grandchild, Sir Edmund Black, in "Part Two: The Land". When we decided to merge the two albums, the storyline was lost. *Lord Of The Night* does not hold to the original concept.

"The Last Stand" is an anti-tradition, anti-conformism song. The lyrics pretty much speak for themselves. This is the only song that I re-wrote from scratch after we changed our plans for the album. The original was a power/heavy metal song that reflected Sir Black leaving the underground and facing the society that he kept alive, though it treated him as an abomination.

"Cease Fire," first written in 1996 during the Israeli Grapes of Wrath aggression against Lebanon, was later re-arranged and expanded during the second war against Lebanon in 2006. This song emphasizes how the Arab and international community remained silent and turned their backs against the Zionist massacres. It accuses the international and Arab world of being the actual "murderers" of our Lebanese children because of their silence.

We re-arranged and re-recorded "Am I Black," our 1998 single, but the meaning of the song is still the same. It was my first composition ever. It is actually a Christian theology song, written back when I was a believer. It remains a song of hope and aspiration.

"Rip It Off" is a personal song. I was criticized by the metal community because I sang "emotional" classic and hard rock cover songs with [my other band] Communion. This song was my reply—a "FUCK YOU" song against conformism and society.

AN UNUSUAL HEAVY METAL LOVE STORY
March 2013

I t's a Sunday night at El Sawy Culture Wheel—a good place to catch a heavy metal show in Cairo—and the twenty-seven-year-old Sherine Amr is bellowing the lyrics to "The World Is Rising," a tense, churning song of war and triumph. Moshing is common at El Sawy gigs, but tonight the crowd watches politely, nodding so slightly that only a fellow metalhead might recognize the gesture as headbanging. This happens every time the band plays in Egypt, Amr says. It's as though listeners can't quite grasp that a woman's voice could be so harsh.

Amr's heavy-metal love story is, at least on the surface, textbook: when she was sixteen, someone loaned her a Metallica CD and she never looked back. But this was in Egypt, in 2001, four years after security forces raided the homes of nearly a hundred metalheads, arresting them on spurious occult charges. Most were released within a fortnight, but the chilling effect on Egypt's metal scene lasted nearly a decade. Western heavy metal stormed the Middle East in the late nineteen-eighties and early nineteen-nineties, taking over the airwaves just as it did in America and Europe. But in heavily Islamic nations like Lebanon, Morocco, and Egypt, the genre's popularity was followed by crackdowns, arrests, and government bans, leaving nascent heavy-metal communities in shreds.

Amr has a warm, kind face framed by long, curly brown hair; it would be obvious to say she doesn't look like a hardcore metalhead. Nevertheless, she's one of many musicians in the region working to rebuild metal's strength. Like other girls, she began studying music early on, learning to sing at age six. But when she picked up a guitar at nineteen, it was to play metal. At the time, she was struggling with career plans after dropping out of law school; her family expected she would marry and start a family. Hoping to discourage her new hobby, Amr's mother forbade her to play music with men, prompting the teen to form Egypt's first all-female heavy-metal band, Massive Scar Era. She recruited a classically trained violinist, Nancy Mounir, early on, establishing the band's signature mix of crushing riffs and Arabian-inflected melodies.

As Egypt's metal scene recovered, Massive Scar Era built a following in seaside Alexandria. And tensions at home increased for Amr. "My older sister thought that I'm turning into a satanist and even [told] my mom to get a sheikh to read the Koran for me, to make sure that if I'm haunted by the devil, it will go away," she says, punctuating the statement with a laugh. Her family's attitude changed in 2010, when the director Ahmed Abdalla asked the band to be in *Microphone*, his film exploring Alexandria's underground scene. Amr was shocked by the invitation, but eager to tell the band's story—and disprove local rumors that Massive Scar Era was only popular because it was an all-women band. Again, Amr's mom protested, prompting Abdalla to blur the band's scenes. But when Amr's family saw *Microphone*, "They understood what kind of pressure they put on me for playing the music I like," she says. "That movie was a turning point in my life." They've been supportive ever since.

Women heavy-metal musicians are increasingly common in the West, whereas in the Middle East and North Africa, you can typically count a country's female metal performers on one hand—but that's changing. As the region's young women fight for equal political footing, they're also cropping up in bands that play extreme music. As they're raising their voices, they're also finding acceptance—and friction—in unexpected places. "Metal is loud, and when people judge from the outside, one might perceive it as motivation or encouragement towards aggression, violence, anger, or loss of personal faith," says Heidi Habib, founder of Dubai's one-woman heavy-metal outfit, Hera, who sports long, dark hair, dramatic makeup, and tattoos. "For myself, it's just a plea to be heard."

Although many of these women's families dug in their heels at the idea of their daughters joining the metal fray, they also arguably paved the way. Amr was raised in a religious but relatively liberal household, where she was encouraged to sing and play piano. Hadeel Ladki, the singer for Lebanon's Testrogen, grew up in a similarly liberal Muslim household in Kuwait, where her parents urged her to learn the piano. Ladki's father frowned on her budding interest in singing until he saw that it wasn't interfering with her academics. Ladki, who wears a ponytail and little makeup during gigs, says metal offered her a respite from Kuwait's "closed and uptight" culture, and allowed her to set herself apart from other Kuwaiti girls, who "tend to be very shallow ... most of them wear the hijab, which is a sign of them choosing the religious path, but you can tell by the way they talk that they were forced into it."

Even non-religious women who join the region's metal bands can face serious challenges. In Iran, home to the metal band Frosted Leaves, it's illegal to perform heavy metal and for women to perform at all—two strikes against the band's vocalist, who goes by the pseudonym Elina and is obscured in band photos to evade arrest. Elina is an anomaly even among the region's lady metalheads: she was raised in a secular household where everyone loved Metallica and Guns N' Roses, including her mother. Despite Iran's laws, her parents let her choose whether to join a metal band.

Some metal fans in the Middle East and North Africa are slowly coming around to the idea of female performers, but the West has had little exposure to them. That, too, may change: Massive Scar Era toured America briefly in 2011 and makes its SXSW debut this week. Some Westerners will have to hastily rearrange their preconceived notions. "There's this sense that Muslim women are naïve, that they are controlled by their men, that they don't have a voice," says the comedian Zahra Noorbakhsh, whose work explores growing up Muslim in America. Haleh Esfandiari, the director of the Middle East Program at the Woodrow Wilson International Center for Scholars in Washington, D.C., and the author of books on Middle Eastern women's rights, says regular exposure to Muslim and Middle Eastern women is the only way people's minds will change. She's glad to see the region's young women finding their voices, particularly relative to the Arab Spring, but she fears what new Islamic regimes will do to that freedom. "The danger is, women are being marginalized," she says.

For Amr, the restrictions of President Mohamed Morsi's government have hit home. Shortly after Morsi took office, the Muslim Brotherhood claimed that metal shows at venues like El Sawy are essentially satanic rituals. Amr's face was plastered in local newspapers alongside articles calling her a Satanist. She's suing for defamation. Amr and her fellow musicians don't see any disconnect between their lives as metal performers, as women, and as Muslims. They're looking for chances to show the world that they can be all three—without reprisals. "Our families taught us how to love, how to care, how to be always clean inside out, how to socialize," Ladki says. "But most importantly, they taught us not to use violence in order to express ourselves and be open to other opinions. They taught us to have dreams and ambition, on which we'll build a future. These are the true Islamic basics."

EGYPT'S LATEST IN THE WAR ON METAL
June 2013

It was Friday, May 3, the day after Jeff Hanneman departed for the great gig in the sky. In Hanneman's memory, 24-year-old Safy Averse El Den put on his Slayer t-shirt before heading into downtown Cairo for an afternoon meal with friends at a cafe. Like Safy, the others were dressed in classic metalhead gear: black shirts celebrating Metallica, Opeth, Pink Floyd, and other bands. That's likely what attracted the attention of the men who advanced on them, snatched the food from their table, tossed it in the trash, and then grabbed Safy and his friends. At first, Safy thought they were patrons picking a fight. Then the men identified themselves as police and ordered the group outside.

Safy and five of his friends were arrested that afternoon, including Refaat "Shady" Khaled, Ahmad Hashim Manch, Mahmoud Haggag, Jehan Faisal Mohammed, and Medhat Mohamed Reza Qasim (who goes by "Brutal Mitch"). The officers packed them into police vans and then did something odd: drove them east to the station in Moski, rather than the one closest to downtown Cairo. "They did that in order to take us to a place where no one will be able to reach us," Safy says.

Once they arrived at the station in Moski, the police confiscated everyone's cell phones, money, and identification. They questioned and beat several of Safy's friends, including 18-year-old Jehan, a woman. Some who made the mistake of asking what was going on were tased. Safy kept quiet, knowing what would happen if he didn't.

It got even weirder. The police forced them to put on dark sunglasses and tie black scarves around their faces. Then they took pictures.

The officers didn't tell them what was happening; "they were doing everything they wanted with violence," Safy says. "We were questioned, but it was like, 'Did you go to the court and try to destroy it?' So I answered, 'No, I didn't go there,' and he writes, 'He went to the court and destroyed it.'"

The youths were divided into smaller groups. Most of Safy's friends were taken to Al Darb Al-Ahmar station, but Safy and Ahmed were held Moski's cells overnight. The next morning, they were brought to the Al-Glaa Court, where they were questioned by the Azbakeya Prosecution. That's when the reason behind the arrests began to emerge. The police explained that black bloc protesters had been destroying property in downtown Cairo the day before, but when the police arrived, the demonstrators predictably fled.

The officers told the court that they later caught up with some of the protesters in a cafe, dressed in black. As evidence, they showed the photos of Safy, Ahmed, Jehan and the others masked in black bandanas and sunglasses. The prosecution ordered that they be held for 15 days.

After the hearing, they were taken about a half hour south of Cairo to Tora Prison, notorious for its high-security "Scorpion" block, where ousted Egyptian president Hosni Mubarak and anti-authoritarian blogger Alaa Seif al-Islam are reportedly held. In Tora, Safy and Ahmed discovered they weren't alone. "We met 21 guys exactly like us," he says. Although the beatings and torture decreased once they reached the prison, the men's long hair was shaved off.

When the guards put Safy in his cell, that's when reality set in. "I felt like I should accept my fate, and began to get used to the jail, as it's my home," he says. "I know that they are great liars, and they know how to put you in a place no one can reach you."

On June 6, 2010, Egyptian Internet activist Khaled Mohamed Saeed was sitting in an Alexandria cybercafe when two detectives from the Sidi Gaber police station entered the cafe and arrested him. As the detectives led Saeed to their car, they beat him and smashed him against objects, ultimately killing him, as multiple witnesses later reported.

"They dragged him to the adjacent building and banged his head against an iron door, the steps of the staircase and walls of the building," the cafe's owner, Hassan Mosbah, said in a taped interview. "Two doctors happened to be there and tried in vain to revive him but (the police) continued beating him ... They continued to beat him even when he was dead."

Afterward, the police claimed Saeed had been arrested on charges of theft and weapons possession, that he had resisted arrest, and that he had suffocated while trying to swallow a packet of hashish. More than a year later, the detectives were found guilty of manslaughter and sentenced to seven years in jail.

Egypt's police force dates back to 1805, when leader Muhammad Ali created a small department in Cairo, according to Omar Ashour, who directs the Middle East Graduate Studies Programme at the Institute of Arab and Islamic Studies at the UK's University of Exeter. In the 1850s, this modest police agency became Egypt's Ministry of Interior, which now has more than 1.5 million employees, including officers, soldiers, administrators and more than 300,000 paid informants, Ashour writes in his paper "From Bad Cop to Good Cop: The challenge of Security Sector Reform in Egypt."

The Ministry of Interior's police division contains two sectors: State Security Investigations (SSI) and Central Security Forces (CSF). When Mubarak became Egypt's president in 1981, the SSI had become the country's most powerful police unit, with 100,000 officers and other employees.

It was during the SSI's power heyday when, on January 22, 1997, police burst into the homes of more than 100 metalheads who were settling into their beds for the night. Most of them were regulars at a place called the Baron's Palace, an abandoned villa turned hangout for the city's metalheads. After the arrests, one Egyptian paper claimed the villa was "filled with tattooed, devil-worshipping youths holding orgies, skinning cats, and writing their names in rats' blood on the palace walls," according to Mark Levine, author of *Heavy Metal Islam*.

The "evidence" against these suspects, some as young as 13, included CDs and cassettes, posters, and black t-shirts. They were interrogated on bizarre topics, including pagan rituals and cat-skinning, and spent up to 45 days in jail before a public prosecutor's demands secured their release. The chilling effect on Egypt's metal scene lasted for nearly a decade, and few metalheads who were old enough to know what was happening at the time will discuss it now.

Clearly, Saeed's beating was by no means an isolated incident, but it was one of the factors that sparked Egypt's revolution on January 25, 2011, the country's "Police Day." In the protests that followed, demonstrators stormed SSI buildings and discovered torture rooms and equipment in every last one. They also secured a number of classified police documents: "Even for apolitical Egyptians, the sheer volume and graphic detail of the released files were shocking," Ashour writes. Although the SSI's reputation for brutality was well known, "From these documents, it becomes clear that the mandate of the SSI was almost exclusively focused on subduing, neutralizing, annihilating or co-opting dissent."

Since the revolution—and particularly since president Muhamed Morsi took office last June—the national conversation in Egypt has turned to police reform, with proposals from civilian groups, the Ministry of the Interior, political organizations, and even the police themselves. "Many [officers] are in need of psychological rehabilitation. The revolution broke some of them, while others became more brutal and violent ... Both situations are equally bad," Egyptian parliamentarian Tamer Makki told Ashour in an interview. But reforming Egypt's deeply entrenched practices will take time, not least because the Muslim Brotherhood's approach to the problem is "gradual ... not revolutionary," Ashour writes.

Despite gestures toward democracy, Morsi and the Muslim Brotherhood's leadership has sparked more protests. In January, near the second anniversary of Egypt's revolution, alleged black bloc protests cropped up in Cairo, Alexandria and near the Suez Canal. At the same time, the Black Bloc Egypt Facebook page appeared.

It wasn't long before public prosecutor Talaad Abdallah ordered Egypt's police to detain anyone suspected of participating in such protests; he even encouraged citizens to arrest members of this so-called "organized group that participates in terrorist acts." In early May, just days after Safy and his friends were arrested, an Egyptian court sentenced six other young men to five and a half years in prison for participating in black bloc activities, Reuters reported.

Within a day of their arrest, friends and family learned that that Safy, Ahmed, Jehan, and the others were in jail. One of their friends, Mahmoud El-Kady, launched a Facebook page so he could rally others to stand outside the courthouse during his friends' upcoming hearings. The arrests were particularly troubling for Mahmoud: the only reason he wasn't with them that afternoon in the cafe was that was studying for his upcoming engineering exams.

Safy is a tourism guidance student at Ain Shams University; Ahmed is studying graphic design aimed at advertising and promotion. All six of Mahmoud's friends were detained just days before they were scheduled to take their end-of-term exams, a fact that weighed heavily on Mahmoud when

I first spoke to him a few days after the arrests.

"If they are kept more than this they will miss their final exams," he says. "We are working on making their colleges give them [an extension] but still no one knows how things are going. We don't understand. Even the lawyers don't seem to actually understand ... It's heavy; my friends are kept in jail for something they didn't do."

Aly Adel, a friend of Safy's, is a human-rights lawyer with experience defending others against similar black bloc allegations. He quickly became involved in Safy's case, one of several lawyers who represented the group in court. When I asked Aly about the news reports covering these protests, he scoffed. The police have invented "a black secret organization scenario [so they] have a legal reason to arrest" people, he says. The pictures and news reports may show people dressed in black who are damaging property, but that doesn't mean they belong to an organized criminal protest group, he says.

The group appeared at the North Cairo Primary Court on Tuesday, May 7, where their attorneys argued that they were being held without cause and convinced the court to let everyone go. The judge ordered their release, but the prosecutors immediately appealed, forcing the youths to return to Tora.

If this were an article about an American police-brutality and wrongful-detention case, I would be obligated to call the police department and the jail and give them a chance to tell their side of the story, even if they only said, "no comment." The Egyptian police, apparently, are another matter. I attempted to reach them, both directly and via Interpol, but my attempts went unanswered. Likewise, emails to the Muslim Brotherhood in Egypt—which has gone so far as to hire a public spokesman, Yasser Mehrez, to talk to the press—fell on silence. Several of my Egyptian sources told me it was essentially impossible to reach the police, let alone get them to talk about situations like these.

Following the January 2011 revolution, Egypt's police force has continued to suffer a reputation problem, though for slightly different reasons. Instead of being out on the streets in force, they have withdrawn, a decision that has left the streets "increasingly lawless," writes BBC reporter Shaimaa Khalil. Khalil was allowed inside one of Egypt's police academies, where new cadets claim the force's philosophies and training methods are changing, with a new focus on protecting human rights. But as long as officers remain out of sight, the public feels abandoned—and, at the same time, reports of police brutality continue, Khalil says.

"The media exaggerate some incidents," Dr. General Ahmed Gad Mansour, the new president of Egypt's Police Academy and assistant to the Interior Minister, told Khalil. "I admit there are mistakes but if you keep showing a mistake 24 hours a day for weeks on end and you make programmes and have interviews about it, then that's how you give the impression that it's a huge mistake and that it's systematic. The vast majority of policemen work extremely hard."

The prosecution's appeal was heard Thursday, May 9, this time at the South Cairo Primary Court. After taking arguments from both sides, the court ordered the youths' immediate release. At first, Safy didn't believe it. "I was expecting something like taking us to somewhere else, or something like that," he says.

Even so, before letting them go, the court told them, "Don't do this again," Safy says. "I mean, they still believe that we destroyed [things] and did this stuff."

However, Shady was ordered back to Tora because he'd been carrying a pocketknife when he was arrested. (In post-Mubarak Egypt, carrying a knife for self-defense is pretty normal, Mahmoud says.) Mahmoud changed the photos on the Facebook page to black-and-white images of Shady's face—showing his warm smile and unruly, chin-length curls before they'd been shorn at Tora—with the words "I will not forget you" and "#free_shady."

Shady was finally released May 17, almost a full two weeks after his arrest. Once his friends were free, on Facebook Mahmoud thanked friends and supporters for showing up to the court, and the legal professionals who helped explain what was going on when they didn't understand. But he also said they'd learned a lesson: that injustice surrounds them and can strike anyone at any time. "Each person has to choose" fear or freedom, he wrote. "May God protect us all from our oppressors and injustice."

Already, Safy and his friends are getting back to their lives. Jehan and Shady are engaged to be married. Safy has returned to his band, Metaphorphoses, which struggles to find an audience in a country that still harbors little love for heavy metal. "Our lyrical theme is about inner struggles and human suffering in this country and also in the whole world," he says, "[and] knowing right from wrong and how to fix it." He's unlikely to lack inspiration anytime soon.

Ironically, the police's actions have created more protesters than existed May 3. "We [were] not even connected to politics," Mahmoud tells me. But the arrests changed all that, and now some of Mahmoud's friends are planning a public demonstration June 30 to stand against ongoing police wrongdoing. "Unfortunately we are in a time where you have one of two [choices]," he says. "To sit and watch the political changes or to join and risk yourself."

'HEAVY METAL AFRICA' EXPLORES THE HEAVIER SIDE OF THE CONTINENT

September 2016

Ask a heavy metal fan what they love about the scene, and many will tell you that wherever they travel, they share a common language—a kind of instant fellowship—with other metal fans. While various recent works (including Banger Films' documentary *Global Metal* and Mark Levine's book *Heavy Metal Islam*) have explored the universality of metal culture outside of the West, Africa has largely been ignored. Edward Banchs' new book, *Heavy Metal Africa*, digs deep into what makes Africa's metal bands unique, as well as what they share with headbangers around the world.

The book, out via Word Association Publishers in late September, sees the author visit metal communities in several sub-Saharan and island regions of Africa, including South Africa, Botswana, Zimbabwe and Mauritius. Banchs spent five years traveling to the continent, getting to know musicians and exploring the regions they call home. As a result, the book reads partly as a creation myth about how African metal was born, partly as a travelogue that goes well beyond Africa's tourist destinations.

Metal remains an underground, if widespread, subculture across the African continent. Africans who love metal tend to gravitate toward metalcore and thrash, the latter because, according to Banchs, "that's the genre of those who have something they want to get off their chest." As with metal bands around the world, many in Africa are driven to write about the injustices they've witnessed. They're also driven by a desire to break free from mainstream society.

"Metal represents everything that African youth want: an identity that they discovered and cherish, not one that is chosen for them," Banchs says. According to him, many African metalheads fall in love with the music because they see the scene as a way of striking out against a culture that doesn't represent them.

Banchs, who was born in North Carolina to Puerto Rican parents, discovered metal as a teenager. He became fascinated by Africa in early adulthood, ultimately receiving a master's in African studies from the University of London and later interning as a lobbyist on African matters in Washington D.C. His interest in the continent's metal scenes was sparked by a conversation with a friend.

"I had known about metal in a few countries from trips to the continent, but wanted to see where else it was, and how much of a scene existed in various countries," Banchs says. When he returned to Africa, he was blown away by the continent's thriving metal communities.

Heavy Metal Africa reveals just how dedicated the continent's metalheads are. It opens on the gorgeous island of Madagascar, where young musicians create metal bands out of literally nothing. Kazar drummer Lallar built a drum kit out of cardboard; Balafomanga's Newton made one from plastic.

Ragasy, guitarist for Madagascar band INOX, tells Banchs he started playing guitar along to Deep Purple and Black Sabbath in the 1970s, but even by the mid-1980s, hard rock and guitars remained hard to come by.

So were legitimate metal T-shirts, Banchs writes: "Most of the T-shirts were homemade or bootlegged versions shipped in and sold on street markets. Misspelling of band names, inaccurate album covers and lyrics scrawled on the back that had nothing to do with the associated album on the front were common ... but the Malagasy metal fans who were fortunate to own a few did not care."

Partly because of the way they dress—in black T-shirts and pants, or in studded leather—African metal bands have faced false accusations of Satanism and witchcraft. South Africa had its own version of the Satanic Panic in the 1980s; police departments

Stux Daemon, frontman of of Botswana's Wrust, in the video for "Hate 'Em All."

investigated accusations of Satanism, and many young metalheads were hauled in for questioning, Banchs writes. Even when the author toured Africa recently, he was kicked out of a store in Kenya and mobbed by a hostile group of teenagers in Madagascar because of his Darkest Hour hoodie, which features a grinning demonic goat across the back.

However, that same Satanic Panic inadvertently imported metal into some places where the music was difficult to find. One public speaker, former police officer John Seale, would play metal albums to illustrate what Africa's youth should avoid. "He did us a tremendous favor by what he was doing. He went to great lengths to find these bands!" Groinchum's Christo Bester tells Banchs.

While some musicians were accused of Satanism, others have faced trouble for airing social problems. In Madagascar, Black Wizard made a video for its song "Land of Doom" that depicted the extreme poverty of a neighborhood near band member Nary's house. After the video aired on television, police officers came to Nary's gate, scolding him for revealing the nation's destitute regions.

Over time, African nations have built up their own metal histories, with seminal bands who helped create regional scenes and new generations that carry the torch. In a few places, heavy metal touchstones have entered the mainstream. Madagascar's Apost released a doomsday single, "Apokolipsy," which has become a staple cover tune for other bands—and is often played at weddings there.

But in other places, such as South Africa, metal has remained firmly underground—and metalheads told Banchs they prefer it that way. After apartheid, "We had sanctions, so there were a lot things we couldn't get in South Africa at that time, and [because of the sanctions] a real 'do-it-yourself' culture developed. There was a real brotherhood in the subculture," says Total Chaos' Jay R.

To metal fans who grew up with Western metal, the concept of African metal may seem strange, but Balafomanga's Newton points out that metal ultimately belongs to Africa. "Rock music started here," he says. "It is not Western culture or European culture. It is our culture."

EGYPT'S MASSIVE SCAR ERA SHREDS A WHOLE NEW SOUND

October 2016

L ooking at Cherine Amr, you wouldn't guess she's the frontwoman for one of Egypt's best-known metal bands. She loves wearing colorful clothing, and her guitar bears a Cartoon Network logo. But when she opens her mouth and the death growls rumble out, there's no mistaking her voice.

Amr and close friend Nancy Mounir founded Massive Scar Era (often shortened to Mascara) in 2005 and released their first EP, *Reincarnation*, in 2006. The pair met at a jazz concert in Alexandria, Egypt, and quickly bonded. Amr had been wanting to launch a musical project, but her conservative Muslim family said she could only be in bands with other women, so she was on the lookout for potential bandmates. The pair later relocated to Cairo, and last year Amr moved to Vancouver, British Columbia while Mounir stayed in Cairo. Massive Scar

Era's latest EP, 30 Years, which dropped in August, was recorded across continents and time zones.

Each day, Amr and Mounir would record new pieces of the album and send the files to one another to build upon. It didn't always work out. "Internet in Egypt is not always reliable, so I would go to bed after pressing 'upload' for some files, and the next morning, I would see my least favorite word: 'error,'" Mounir says.

But the result is a stunning four-song collection that explores life in North Africa and the West. The first track, "Alive," opens with rollicking drums, guitar, and Mounir's soaring violin; it's a celebration of survival and success, driven by Amr's guttural roars and clean vocals.

"I wrote it thinking about Nancy and me going through this journey," Amr says. "I wrote it while I was still in Egypt, and I think my body needed a positive reinforcement and encouragement to carry on."

When I first interviewed Amr and Mounir in 2013, Egypt was in a post-Arab Spring state of turmoil following a 2011 revolution that prompted longtime President Hosni Mubarak to flee the country. Mohamed Morsi, who was aligned with the Muslim Brotherhood, was elected to the Egyptian presidency in 2012.

His rise to power was a huge blow to women's rights even though he served for little more than a year before being ousted in a coup. He was lat-

Cherine Amr and Nancy Mounir of Egypt/Canada's Massive Scar Era. Photo courtesy the band.

er charged with numerous crimes, including killing protesters and espionage. Former Defense Minister Abdel Fattah el-Sisi became Egypt's president in 2014. Although el-Sisi's presidency has been more popular among Egyptian people, Amr continued to find the country unlivable.

"The streets in Cairo were getting more aggressive due to the economic problems the country was facing. Everybody was waiting for a fight to jump in to release their anger. It was crazy!" says Amr. Between the political scene and the censorship struggles she faced at work, she decided it was time to leave. "I needed to run away! Save myself and save my dreams."

Before she left in 2015, Amt was working for an art incubator called Garaad where she regularly fought Egypt's censorship committee to help filmmakers, musicians, radio producers, and graphic novelists market and distribute their work. Amr's solo work—along with many other musicians' works—couldn't be released in Egypt because of censorship restrictions that forbid songs from discussing religion or politics, she says.

At El Sawy Culture Wheel, a club in Cairo where Massive Scar Era and other metal bands regularly performed, the powers-that-be were similarly strict. "There is this woman [who worked at the club] who always silently comes in and takes a look at us … just to make sure we aren't wearing shorts or revealing clothing," Amr says. In 2009, she organized a music festival where a Swedish band arrived to perform in dresses and shorts in the ultra-hot Egyptian summertime. The woman told them they would have to change into more modest clothing before going onstage.

Metal bands like Massive Scar Era face numerous problems in Egypt in part because record distributors are reluctant to work with metal; it's often considered an untouchable genre in the region.

"The genre itself has been used for years to distract the public from major political events in the country," Amr says. Every time there's unrest, officials will plant the seed in Egyptian media that "evil Satanic bands are trying to take over our children's minds," she says.

Amr explores her drive to leave Egypt in "Despite My Will," the second track on 30 Years, a sultry, jazzy tune that turns to rage at the choruses. In Arabic, she sings about not being able to cope with the path she's on, about confused thoughts, about rejecting life as it was before she left.

"Despite My Will" is followed by the melancholy, nostalgic title track, which was the first song Amr wrote after moving to Vancouver in April of 2015. To compose the song, Amr and Mounir swapped roles; Amr wrote the string arrangements, while Mounir wrote the guitar lines to support the vocals and violin. The lyrics speak of the past, of someone who's no longer wanted, of empty rooms. It's intentionally unclear whether Amr is singing about a person or about the homeland she left behind.

The final song on 30 Years, "The Fairest of All," takes its cues from the poetry of Arabic writer Al-Mutanabbi, who lived in Egypt more than 1,000 years ago but faced some of the same restrictions artists there face today. "He always wrote praising the kinds of countries he lived in, in return for money and gifts, but at the same time, he was very aware that he was doing it for money, and he was very honest about it," Amr says. Al-Mutanabbi was ultimately killed by a man he directly insulted in a poem.

After living in Vancouver for a year and a half and taking on a role with the Vancouver Fringe Festival, Amr says she feels very welcome in the West. "The freedom, how easygoing the people are, it's really less stressful," she says. "I feel younger and happier."

Amr is hoping that her relocation to North America will bring Massive Scar Era to a wider audience. The band performed at SXSW in 2013 and hopes to do so again next year. Mounir came to Canada this summer to visit and embark on a brief tour to bring the band's music to new audiences. They still get some pushback—audience members often said they weren't expecting such intense, aggressive music from Amr and Mounir.

Although Amr hopes Mounir will want to join her in Canada, Mounir says she'll remain in Cairo for now.

"I cannot dare to talk about the political situation in Egypt now because it's quite abstract," Mounir says. "All I can say is that we're still struggling with freedom of expression—some young people are in jail because of a mobile video, [and] the government is allowed to arrest anybody, whether they have a valid reason or not."

TENACITY: AMID WAR, SYRIAN METALHEADS AREN'T GIVING UP

April 2018

Metalhead Monzer Darwish grew up in one of unfriendliest places in the world for heavy metal: Syria. He fell in love with the music as a teenager, and played in a couple of Syrian metal bands, but his final effort to launch a band there was aborted when a suicide bomber destroyed parts of his hometown of Hama in 2013.

He had originally planned to record the next day with a bandmate, but when he arrived, he found widespread destruction. A whole block of buildings had collapsed. Water sprayed from random pipes. Twisted cars lay on their sides, useless. A neighborhood that had been bustling the day before was now empty and abandoned.

Darwish began recording the devastation with his phone and, from that footage, his documentary *Syrian Metal is War* was born. Where many young men picked up guns to protect their families and towns and to keep other factions out, Darwish—who grew up a passionate metalhead in the riverside city of Hama—picked up his camera, instead, to document and protect what remained of Syria's underground heavy metal community in the face of war.

It wasn't the documentary about Syrian metal that Darwish had planned to make. "I always wanted the global metal scene to recognize Syrian metal bands," he told me by email. He wanted to show the world how tenacious Syria's metal communities are and why its musicians and fans don't give up. "Even before the war, I remember being rejected by so many music studios, because they were too afraid to record metal music. So it was never easy."

Metal has long been a taboo form of music in Syria, and musicians have been arrested and harassed by police for their involvement in the scene. But that didn't stop them—and, as the civil war developed, so did underground metal communities, which locals dubbed the new wave of Syrian heavy metal.

Darwish is tall and slender, with dark hair and large brown eyes framed by black-rimmed glasses. He's a self-taught filmmaker who produced a number of film projects before making *Syrian Metal is War*, including several for Syrian foundations and NGOs. His short film about his migration from Syria to Europe took the top prize in an Institute of Global Affairs competition in 2016. He is a skilled storyteller, threading the scenes and interviews in *Syrian Metal is War* together with his narration, in English, spoken in his melodic, reassuring voice.

Darwish discovered heavy metal as a teenager. One hot summer day, he competed in a computer-programming contest. He was wearing shorts to try to keep cool, but when he arrived, the organizers told him he had to change into long pants because there were girls around. Darwish refused, and the organizers kicked him out. A friend found him outside, angry and crying with frustration.

"He gave me his headset," Darwish recalls. "He said, 'Just listen to it; it'll make your anger vanish.'" He put on the headphones and heard the ballistic sounds of Metallica's "Battery" pulsing in his ears.

"Time froze for me," he says. He asked his friend: "What is this music?"

Back at home, Darwish sought out heavy metal wherever he could. He discovered that his music instructor, who was teaching him to play piano and oud, had a trove of Metallica cassettes, along with other rock and metal albums. The teacher shared his tapes with Darwish, feeding the teen's interest.

Darwish, like metalheads around the world, fell in love with metal for its authenticity and its ability to speak the truth about the world around us. "A music genre that talks about love, hate, politics, philosophy, religion and our existence itself—it was too real and honest, compared to the cheesy love songs I used to hear everywhere," he told me.

Monzer Darwish. Photo courtesy Facebook.

Metal is not new in Syria; Aleppo hosted its first show in 1989, organized by scene patriarch Jack Power and his band, Weltzchmertz. More than 6,000 fans attended that event, and large metal gatherings followed in 1992, 1997 and 2002.

But being a musician in Syria was difficult, even before the war. *In Syrian Metal is War*, Anas and Salim, two musicians who fled Damascus and settled in Beirut, Lebanon, tell stories about run-ins with police. "You get the call, 'You're wanted for the charges of slaughtering cats. You've been under surveillance for a while,'" says Anas, who doesn't wear black or have long hair, so he says he doesn't "look the part." Even Anas' friends who aren't part of the metal scene have asked him—in all seriousness—whether it's true that he drinks cats' blood. "They don't know it's, it's just music!" he says. "It's music that has a little more gain. Case closed."

Not long after Darwish discovered heavy metal, he began learning to play guitar, at 15. He taught himself to play along to Metallica's "Nothing Else Matters," "Wherever I May Roam" and "The Four Horseman" before veering off into more extreme branches of the heavy metal family tree. His bands in Hama included a black-metal band and a doom band. "It was pretty hard to find others to play music with, it was harder to find practicing space, and almost impossible to find a studio that would accept recording our music," The only studio in Syria that recorded metal music on a pro level was the Old Hearth Studio, run by Fadi Massamiri in Damascus, but it is now closed. His bandmates lived in different cities, and traveling became difficult and unsafe once the fighting started.

Some governments fear metal just because it's "Western," Darwish tells me. "Some because of their religious beliefs, and some because they think it's evil. Changing that requires a lot of effort. It's not just about not accepting heavy metal, but about the mentality that leads people to believe they can judge a person because of how he looks like, or because of a musical genre he plays or listens to. That needs to change."

Aleppo was home to a thriving metal scene before the war transformed it into what Darwish describes, in the film, as "the wasteland that was Syria's economical [sic] capital;" the scene then moved to Lattakia, and many metal "refugees" moved with it. The city became a home base for Syria's metal scene, and for planning gigs and recording sessions anywhere metalheads could. Syrian metal legend Bashar Haroum, known for organizing live shows in Syria, was among those who relocated to Lattakia. In late 2013, he was planning another gig, dubbed "Live Under Siege," back in Aleppo. Despite the destruction, a number of coffee shops and underground metal venues survived through the mid-2010s. One of them, Buzz Cafe, hosted the show. But, when the day came for "Live Under Siege," the power went out five minutes before the first band was scheduled to take the stage. A generator eventually arrived and the show got underway, just a few kilometers from an active war zone.

Such gigs are a rare treat, and the turnout for this one was remarkable. As Darwish says in the film, "Metal is our vessel for peace, as well as an escape for the troubled." It was also the last time the filmmaker played guitar onstage.

During his visit to Aleppo, Darwish spent time with his friend Matt, the guitarist for Chaos. Matt wears a knitted beanie, and he has a beard and kind eyes that carry a touch of sadness. Inside an apartment, he showed Darwish windows pocked with bullet holes, and another window that cracked after a bomb exploded nearby. Pointing, Matt describes how pedestrians walk calmly along the streets outside his windows. But a few streets away, they dash through crossings where snipers perch overhead. The electricity only comes on for an hour or two a day, at best.

Matt is smiling as he describes the danger and destruction, but underneath, he is nervous, uncomfortable; anyone would be.

Those mixed emotions punctuate the documentary. As Darwish begins to interview college student and new-wave musician Mohammad Dimashqi in Damascus, a bomb drops in the distance, and Dimashqi laughs anxiously. Although musicians are still able to make time to write, record and perform music during the war, dealing with the day-to-day skirmishes is exhausting.

In a studio in Damascus, where the electricity is out, a member of the band Vileden practices riffs by candlelight as mortars explode in the distance. Later, with the power on, a cluster of musicians noodle on their instruments as the building shakes with each mortar blast. They snicker nervously and keep playing.

"The unending symphonies of Damascus are bullets and generators," Darwish says.

When Dimashqi's band was working on a new album, "we'd get to the studio tired, unable to work," he tells Darwish. He and his bandmates would get depressed by the fighting and the news, and had little motivation to make music. "Sometimes you feel like it's not time."

But when they could bring themselves to play music together, it was a comfort, he continues. "We'd forget. We'd forget for at least two or three hours that there's something happening outside, that something might be happening beneath us. We're sitting together, playing, happy that we're making something."

Even as the documentary describes the specific struggles faced by metalheads in the Middle East, it underscores the similarities among metalheads around the world. They band together in makeshift spaces, smoke, play guitars, keep each other company.

For a variety of reasons, metalheads are kindred spirits. Young people anywhere experience rage, frustration and feelings of defeat; it's part of being a teenager or young adult, Darwish says. Metal is a benign way to express those feelings, and it offers community among metalheads at the same time. Young people may ask themselves whether their challenges mean they are alone in the world. "'No, you're not,' metal says back," Darwish says.

During wartime, those feelings of anger, frustration and defeat are intensified, he says. Metal music becomes even more of a comfort, even a necessity. Still, as he traveled through Syria and Lebanon, he was surprised by the way daily experiences of war have created a unifying experience for the metalheads he talked with.

"We all have a reference as to what an AK sounds like, a mortar, or an explosion. We can tell the difference between a MiG and a Sukhoi before we can even see it," Darwish says. "The world can be so surreal sometimes. And yet, despite all of that, everyone still manages to maintain a unique voice and create unique music."

Late in the film, Darwish heads to Homs, about 50 kilometers south of Hama, where few neighborhoods remain intact. Whole districts lie in ruins, the streets piled with rubble and abandoned cars. It makes you wonder who will clean it all up—who will help the city rebuild? How long will it remain this way? Seven years after it started, the war in Syria shows no signs of letting up In February of 2018, UNICEF, the United Nations agency for children, issued a blank statement after mass casualties of children were reported in Eastern Ghouta and Damascus, saying, "No words will do justice to the children killed, their mothers, their fathers and their loved ones."

Five months after the suicide bombing that sparked *Syrian Metal is War,* Darwish returns to Hama and meets with his former bandmate, B. Nord, only to find that he has traded his guitar for a military rifle.

"I never thought I'd pick up arms or learn to use a weapon, at least not in this way," Nord says. "But after the explosion in our village and after all I've seen, a group of guys from the village and myself had to learn how to use weapons, to first protect ourselves, our village, and make sure that what happened doesn't repeat itself."

"Do you think it would be possible to carry a guitar again?" Darwish asks.

"I don't think this is the time to carry a guitar," Nord replies.

Soon after that visit, Darwish left Syria, taking one of countless rubber rafts across the Mediterranean with all of his documentary footage in tow. Much of it survived the journey. He eventually settled in Amsterdam with his wife, who's also Syrian. But Darwish didn't have the money or equipment to assemble the film. A Swiss metalhead, Marie Alice Riley, launched a crowdfunding campaign on wemakeit.com, ultimately raising more than €7,400 for Darwish to begin editing.

Riley heard about the documentary through news reports and reached out to Darwish, offering to arrange the fundraiser. At first, he was reluctant, saying, "I'm not used to asking for help." So many people supported the idea, however, that he eventually agreed. "If not for the crowdfunding campaign, it would've been impossible for me to edit the film," he says.

Despite two years in the Netherlands, Darwish hasn't connected with the local metal scene yet. He has been busy finishing the film, learning Dutch, and pursuing other film projects. There are many times when he gets homesick for Hama—not the chaos and violence, but the life he had before the civil war. He misses his parents, who are still there. He misses his house, his cat, the food of home. "Most of my memories and dreams consist of the days before 2011," he says. "I do wish I could get back, but it's way more complicated than that."

He also misses the metal community he left behind, and carries with him the Syrian metalheads, both in Syria and in the diaspora, who continue to do everything they can to keep the scene alive.

"I think it's inevitable that we keep striving for it. It's a facet of our identity to some extent," he says. "I find it inspiring. In fact, so inspiring I made a whole documentary about it with almost nothing! The Syrian way."

PUBLISHING NOTES

"The Heavy Metal Witch Hunt Lives On" was first published in *PopMatters*, June 3, 2012.

"Interview: Bassem Deaïbess of Lebanon's Blaakyum" was first published in *Invisible Oranges,* February 9, 2012.

"An Unusual Heavy-Metal Love Story" was first published in the *New Yorker,* March 13, 2013.

"Egypt's Latest in the War on Metal" was first published in *Invisible Oranges,* June 26, 2013.

"Edward Banchs' New Book, 'Heavy Metal Africa,' Explores the Heavier Side of the Continent" was first published in *Noisey*, September 9. 2016.

"Egypt's Female-Fronted Metal Band Massive Scar Era Shreds a Whole New Sound" was first published in *Bitch*, October 25, 2016.